JAN 11

WEEKLY **WR** READER®
EARLY LEARNING LIBRARY

Things with Wings

THE LIFE CYCLE OF A
MOTH

by JoAnn Early Macken

Reading consultant: Susan Nations, M.Ed.,
author/literacy coach/consultant in literacy development

Please visit our web site at: **www.earlyliteracy.cc**
For a free color catalog describing **Weekly Reader®** Early Learning Library's
list of high-quality books, call 1-877-445-5824 (USA) or 1-800-387-3178 (Canada).
Weekly Reader® Early Learning Library's fax: (414) 336-0164.

Library of Congress Cataloging-in-Publication Data

Macken, JoAnn Early, 1953-
    The life cycle of a moth / by JoAnn Early Macken.
        p. cm. — (Things with wings)
    Includes index.
    ISBN 0-8368-6384-4 (lib. bdg.)
    ISBN 0-8368-6391-7 (softcover)
    1. Moths—Life cycles—Juvenile literature. I. Title.
  QL544.2.M22   2006
  595.78—dc22   2005026609

This edition first published in 2006 by
Weekly Reader® Early Learning Library
A Member of the WRC Media Family of Companies
330 West Olive Street, Suite 100
Milwaukee, WI 53212 USA

Managing editor: Dorothy L. Gibbs
Art direction: Tammy West
Photo research: Diane Laska-Swanke

Photo credits: Cover, © Mark Schneider/Visuals Unlimited; pp. 5, 7, 9, 19 © Hans Christoph
Kappel/naturepl.com; p. 11 © Ingo Arndt/naturepl.com; p. 13 © Pete Oxford/naturepl.com; p. 15
© James P. Rowan; p. 17 © Richard Day/Daybreak Imagery; p. 21 © Leroy Simon/Visuals Unlimited

Printed in the United States of America

1 2 3 4 5 6 7 8 9 10 09 08 07 06

Note to Educators and Parents

Reading is such an exciting adventure for young children! They are beginning to integrate their oral language skills with written language. To encourage children along the path to early literacy, books must be colorful, engaging, and interesting; they should invite the young reader to explore both the print and the pictures.

Things with Wings is a new series designed to help children read about fascinating animals, all of which have wings. In each book, young readers will learn about the life cycle of the featured animal, as well as other interesting facts.

Each book is specially designed to support the young reader in the reading process. The familiar topics are appealing to young children and invite them to read — and re-read — again and again. The full-color photographs and enhanced text further support the student during the reading process.

In addition to serving as wonderful picture books in schools, libraries, homes, and other places where children learn to love reading, these books are specifically intended to be read within an instructional guided reading group. This small group setting allows beginning readers to work with a fluent adult model as they make meaning from the text. After children develop fluency with the text and content, the book can be read independently. Children and adults alike will find these books supportive, engaging, and fun!

— Susan Nations, M.Ed., author, literacy coach, and consultant in literacy development

Young moths hatch from eggs.
The young moths are called
caterpillars. They crawl out
and eat. Most kinds chew
leaves. Some eat fruit or seeds.

egg

caterpillar

5

Moth caterpillars grow fast. As they grow, they shed their skin, or **molt**. Most kinds molt five times. After a caterpillar molts for the last time, it becomes a **pupa**.

To turn into a pupa, most moth caterpillars dig into the ground. Some kinds build cocoons around their bodies. Some cocoons hang from trees. Others rest on the ground.

pupa

9

When a caterpillar turns into a pupa, it grows a hard shell. Inside the shell, it forms wings. Its mouth changes, too.

shell

11

Some pupae come out of the ground. Some come out of cocoons. When they come out, they are moths.

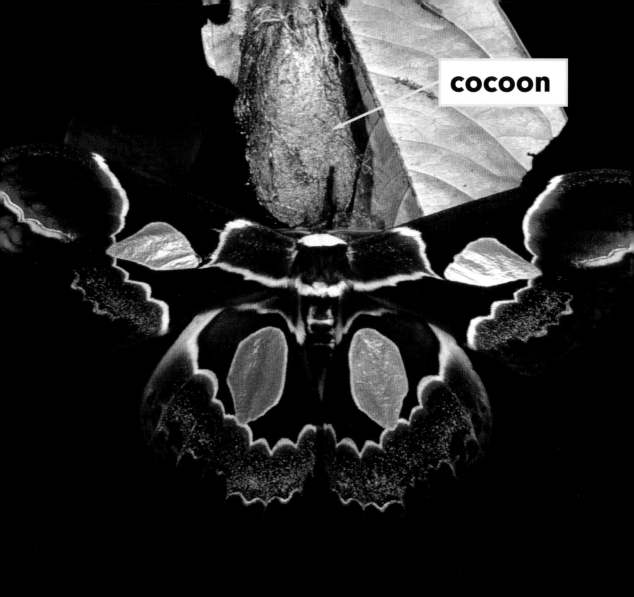

cocoon

Moths have thick bodies. Most moths have two large eyes and two small eyes. All moths have six legs and four wings. They also have two **antennae**, or feelers.

antennae

A moth feeds through a tube called a **proboscis** (pro BAHS iss). It sucks nectar from flowers.

proboscis

17

Most moths are active at night.
During the day, they sleep.
When they rest, most moths
hold their wings flat.

Moth wings are covered with scales. The scales are often brown or gray. Their colors blend in with trees and dry leaves. Many moths live only a few days or weeks.

21

The Life Cycle of a Moth

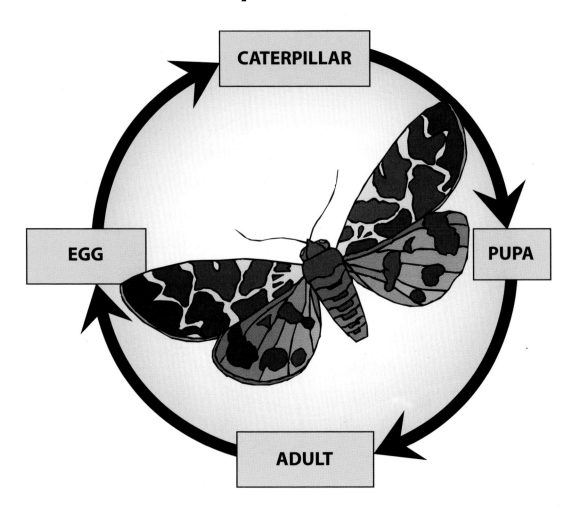

CATERPILLAR

EGG

PUPA

ADULT

Glossary

cocoons — cases that hold insects during the pupa stage

hatches — breaks out of an egg

molt — to shed, or lose, the skin

pupa — an insect in the stage between larva and adult

scales — thin, flat plates on the wings of insects

Index

About the Author

JoAnn Early Macken is the author of two rhyming picture books, *Sing-Along Song* and *Cats on Judy*, and more than eighty nonfiction books for children. Her poems have appeared in several children's magazines. A graduate of the M.F.A. in Writing for Children and Young Adults Program at Vermont College, she lives in Wisconsin with her husband and their two sons.